This book belongs to

. . . .

DANIEL
in the
Lions' Den

First published in Great Britain in 2017

Society for Promoting Christian Knowledge
36 Causton Street, London SW1P 4ST
www.spck.org.uk

Text copyright © Alexa Tewkesbury 2017
Illustrations copyright © Dani Padrón 2017

British Library Cataloguing-in-Publication Data
A catalogue record for this book is available from the British Library

ISBN 978-0-281-07498-3

Typeset by Gill McLean
Printed in Great Britain by Ashford Colour Press

1 3 5 7 9 10 8 6 4 2

Produced on paper from sustainable forests

DANIEL
in the
Lions' Den

Alexa Tewkesbury

Illustrated by Dani Padrón

People to meet, places to go. **Rush, rush**.
Lists to write and jobs to be done.
Busy, busy. I work for the king.

I work very hard indeed. **Phew!**

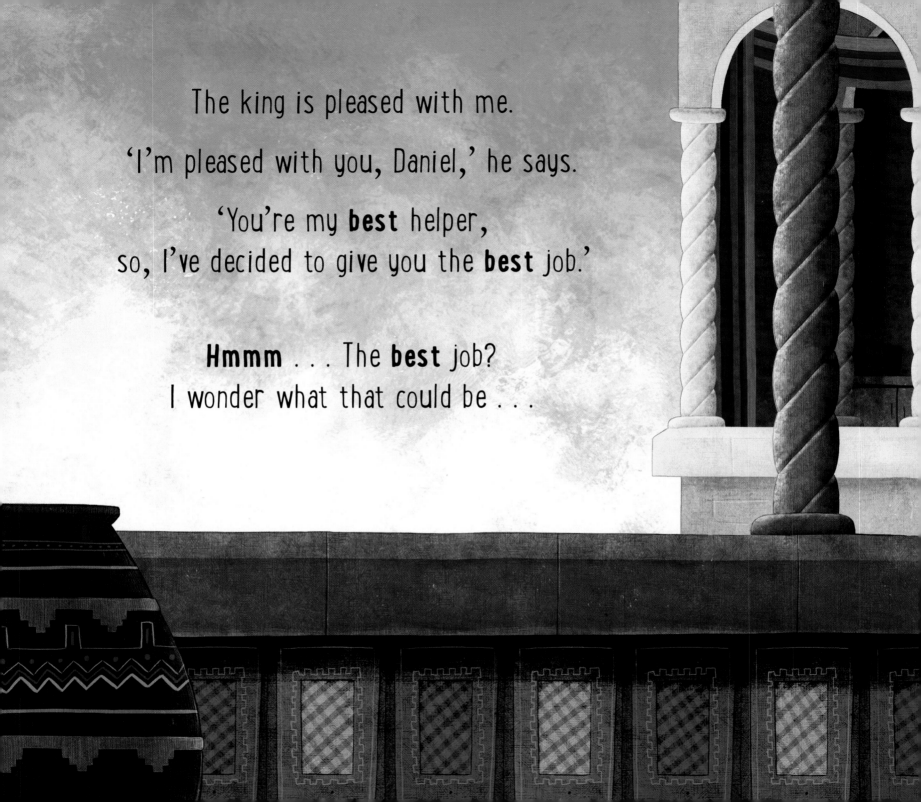

The king is pleased with me.

'I'm pleased with you, Daniel,' he says.

'You're my **best** helper,
so, I've decided to give you the **best** job.'

Hmmm . . . The **best** job?
I wonder what that could be . . .

Will I be in charge of the king's palace?

Will I be in charge of the king's gardens?

No, the **best** job is to be
in charge of the
king's whole kingdom.

But not everyone is excited.
Some people who work for the king are grumpy.

They want the **best** job for **themselves**.

Oh dear. Now I'm in trouble.

Those workers
don't seem to **like** me very much.

The grumpy workers are off to see the king.

'Your majesty,' they say,
'let's have a new law.
A law that says people must **worship only you**.'

The king chuckles.
The king claps his hands.

'**Yes!**
That's a wonderful idea.'

What **terrible** news!

The grumpy workers know I worship God.
Three times a day, **every** day,
I worship God.

I **can't** stop,
I **won't** stop.

I may **work** for the king, but I will **worship** only God.

I **still** pray to God at my window.

The grumpy workers
point at me,
but I **still** talk to God.

Look –
they're running to the king.

Still I don't stop.

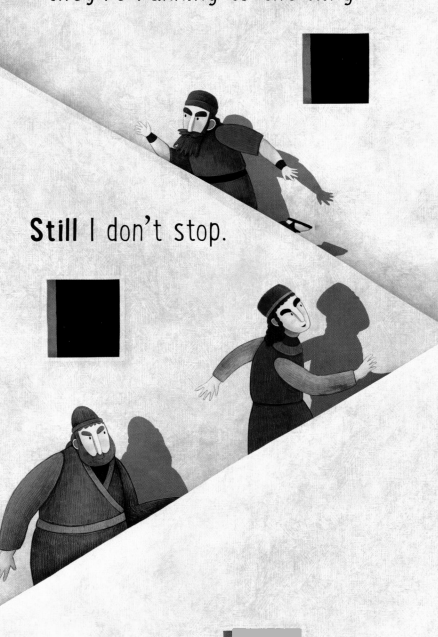

'Your majesty,
Daniel is breaking your new law!

He's not worshipping **you**,
he's worshipping **God**.'

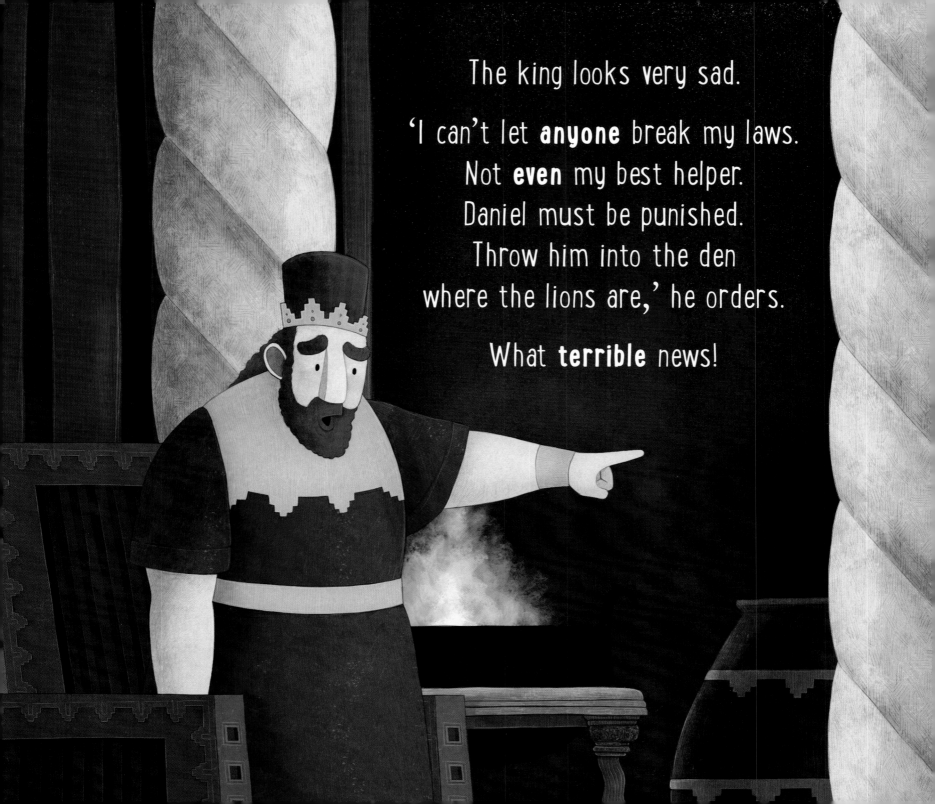

The king looks very sad.

'I can't let **anyone** break my laws.
Not **even** my best helper.
Daniel must be punished.
Throw him into the den
where the lions are,' he orders.

What **terrible** news!

I'm sad, too. Sad and afraid.

Those lions look **hungry**.

'Daniel,' says the king.
'You love God **so much**.
I hope he can **save** you.'

It's **dark** in here. Dark in the den with the lions. Will God save me?

How many **lions** are there?
How many lions' **teeth** are there?
Too many . . . What **terrible** news!

'Daniel!' Is that the **king?**
'I've been worried **all** night, Daniel. Has God **saved** you?'

I can't stop my mouth from **grinning**.
'**Yes!**' I can't keep my mouth from **laughing!**
'**Yes!** God sent an **angel** to shut the lions' jaws.
I'm **safe**. They **couldn't** hurt me.'

The king beams.
'Get my best helper
out of this den,' he orders,
'and get rid of that **silly** new law.
From now on we will **all** worship God.
God, who **saved** Daniel.'

Well . . . what **wonderful** news!

Can you spot the **8 differences** between these two pictures?

Other titles in the series
by Alexa Tewkesbury

Noah and his Ark

978-0-281-07496-9

Jonah and the Whale

978-0-281-07500-3

SPCK

www.spck.org.uk